BRAILLE ALPHABET

A	B	C	D	E	F	G	H	I
J	K	L	M	N	O	P	Q	R
S	T	U	V	W	X	Y	Z	

LOWER CASE ALPHABET

a	b	c	d	e	f	g	h	i
j	k	l	m	n	o	p	q	r
s	t	u	v	w	x	y	z	

COMMUNICATION
ALIKI

GREENWILLOW BOOKS, NEW YORK

MANY THANKS TO JUDITH FINESTONE

Watercolor paints, colored pencils, and a black pen were used for the full-color art. The text type is Symbol Medium; hand lettering was done by the artist. Copyright © 1993 by Aliki Brandenberg. All rights reserved. No part of this book may be reproduced or utilized in any form or by any means, electronic or mechanical, including photocopying, recording, or by any information storage and retrieval system, without permission in writing from the Publisher, Greenwillow Books, a division of William Morrow & Company, Inc., 1350 Avenue of the Americas, New York, NY 10019.   Printed in Hong Kong by South China Printing Company (1988) Ltd.   First Edition
1 2 3 4 5 6 7 8 9 10

Library of Congress Cataloging-in-Publication Data
Aliki.   Communication / by Aliki.   p.   cm.
Summary: Discusses the many different kinds of
communication and the functions they serve.
ISBN 0-688-10529-7 (trade). ISBN 0-688-11248-X (lib. bdg.)
1. Communication — Juvenile literature.   [1. Communication.]
I. Title.   P91.2.A44   1993   302.2 — dc20   91-48156   CIP   AC

COMMUNICATION

Communication is sharing knowledge.

It is telling news.

It is expressing feelings...

and being heard.

IT TAKES **TWO** TO COMMUNICATE

One to say it.

One to listen...

and respond.

You'll both be glad you did.

WE COMMUNICATE THROUGH LANGUAGE

We speak words.

We listen to words.

We write words.

We read words.

 We all need to express ourselves.

Right.

B U T . . .

Before babies learn to speak words, they communicate in other ways.
Oh, oh. I don't think you like this...
FFFFF
Spinach is horrible, but I don't know how to tell you yet.
I want Hunky Monkey, but I can't say it.
Is this the one you want?
If we look and listen, we can understand.
WAAA
Waaa
WAAA
I'm sleepy, but I can't explain it.
I'll bet you're sleepy.
zz
Understood babies sleep happily.

purrr

THERE ARE OTHER WAYS

Before early people learned to write, they communicated through pictures.

Even today, we use signs and symbols to communicate.

We communicate without words:

We touch, hug, and kiss. We applaud.

We stamp, push, pull, hit, and kick.

If we can't speak someone's language, we use body language.

Artists communicate through pictures, dancers through dance, musicians through music, ♪ writers and poets through words.

Other means of communication:

letters | newspapers | books

magazines | telephone | codes | radio | television

ANIMALS COMMUNICATE, TOO

*I'm hungry!

*Welcome home!

*You're too close!

*This is fun!

BUT HUMAN BEINGS ARE THE GREAT COMMUNICATORS

And we all need someone to tell.

TELL ME

YOU ASKED FOR IT

SOME THINGS ARE EASY
TO COMMUNICATE

Hi, Grandma! You should have seen what happened in school today. Our bunny escaped and nobody could find her any where...

Grandma must like to hear from Nikki, too.

SOME THINGS ARE HARD TO SAY

BUT IT'S A RELIEF WHEN YOU SAY THEM

FEELINGS are hard to communicate.

MY DIARY

Sometimes when a feeling is fresh,
it is hard to explain it to someone else.
So I communicate with myself.
I write it in my diary.
It helps me understand what is troubling me.

After that, I feel better.
Writing makes things clear.
It makes it easier to explain to someone else.
Sometimes just writing it down makes
the hurt go away.

But my diary is for fun and news, too —
and for remembering.

 It's good practice
writing, too!

ARE YOU LISTENING?

FEEDBACK

I need feedback. When you tell somebody something, it's nice to have a response.
You're right. There's nothing worse than talking to a brick wall. Some people are like that.
Otherwise, you feel lonely— you feel as if nobody cares.
Jack never gives me any feedback. I say, "Hi, Jack, it's a great day," and he acts as if he didn't hear.
My dad does that sometimes. Yesterday I wanted to tell him about swimming class, but he was buried in his newspaper.
Yeah. It's nice to share things. For instance, you tell me and I'll tell you and then we'll know how the other feels.

Répondez, s'il vous plaît! *
Have you ever read Treasure Island? It's the greatest book! But scary!
FIFTEEN MEN ON A DEAD MAN'S CHEST. YO HO HO AND A BOTTLE OF RUM! GULP!
Remember when Jim Hawkins hides from Long John Silver in the apple barrel?
I had to get way under the covers, I was so scared!
But if you want to LAUGH — remember Stuart Little?
How he got caught up in the window shade?
And all his adventures — driving around the countryside.
Ha. Ha.
Books are great, and it's fun when you can share them, too.
Oh, by the way - next week we're driving up to Kouchi Falls. I'll tell you all about it.
Everybody needs some RSVP.
* That's French for feedback! Ha.

THANK YOU FOR TELLING ME

PEN PALS

THERE IS ALWAYS A WAY TO COMMUNICATE

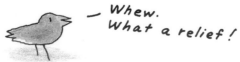

Sometimes a book can communicate
your feelings to you.

IF YOU DON'T COMMUNICATE, YOU MAY NEVER KNOW

RACHEL LETS IT ALL HANG OUT

HAPPY BIRTHDAY

DID YOU HEAR?

And now I'll sing you a song,
then I'll tell you a story, and a poem,
then I'll announce the latest news,
then I'll answer your questions...
then ... hey, where are you?
Where is everybody?
I need to do it with somebody!

COMMUNICATION
*is the back and forth of telling
and listening and responding,
so you know you are not alone.*

UPPER CASE ALPHABET

A	B	C	D	E	F	G	H	I
J	K	L	M	N	O	P	Q	R
S	T	U	V	W	X	Y	Z	

SIGN LANGUAGE ALPHABET

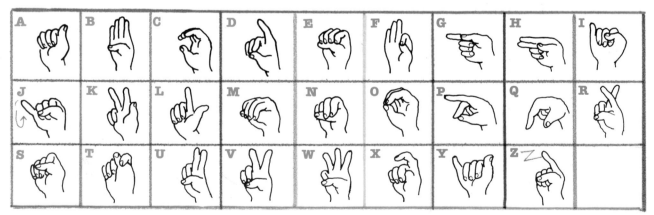